GOA kids | GOATS OF ANARCHY

THE GOAT
WITH MANY COATS

Brimming with creative inspiration, how-to projects, and useful information to enrich your everyday life, Quarto Knows is a favorite destination for those pursuing their interests and passions. Visit our site and dig deeper with our books into your area of interest: Quarto Creates, Quarto Cooks, Quarto Homes, Quarto Lives, Quarto Drives, Quarto Explores, Quarto Gifts, or Quarto Kids.

First Published in 2017 by Walter Foster Jr., an imprint of The Quarto Group.
6 Orchard Road, Suite 100, Lake Forest, CA 92630, USA.
T (949) 380-7510 F (949) 380-7575 www.QuartoKnows.com

Walter Foster Jr. titles are also available at discount for retail, wholesale, promotional, and bulk purchase. For details, contact the Special Sales Manager by email at specialsales@quarto.com or by mail at The Quarto Group, Attn: Special Sales Manager, 401 Second Avenue North, Suite 310, Minneapolis, MN 55401 USA.

ISBN: 978-1-63322-333-2

Content development by Saskia Lacey
Illustrated by Jill Howarth

Printed in China
10 9 8 7 6 5 4 3

GOA *kids* | GOATS OF ANARCHY

THE GOAT

WITH MANY COATS

By **LEANNE LAURICELLA** with *Saskia Lacey*

Illustrated by **JILL HOWARTH**

This is the true story of a little orphan goat.

It was a December night, cold and bright, when Prospect was born. The trees rustled with winter air and stars shone through the falling snow.

As tiny as a teacup, Prospect weighed just one pound.
He had a pink, heart-shaped nose, one droopy ear,
and legs that wobbled when he walked.

In the little goat's first hours, he was lonely; his family was nowhere to be found. One of his ears drooped sadly.

But Prospect was lucky—one day, a young woman came to the farm. She wanted to adopt him! During the long drive home, his new mom held him close.

For the first time, Prospect felt safe and loved.

The little goat's new home felt BIG. Tables and chairs towered above him. It was all a bit scary.

But then, Prospect met Piney, a kind and wise house pig. Piney kept Prospect company on his first night. The two friends snuggled by the fire.

The next morning, chilly air seeped under doors and through windowpanes. The little goat was cold. Prospect was just a baby, and his coat was not thick enough to keep him warm.

His mom had an idea. She would give him another coat to wear!

As soon as his coat was zipped and buttoned, Prospect felt like a new goat. His floppy ear straightened. His legs were more sure. The coat made Prospect feel strong.

Prospect adored his coat, and soon got another. And then another! He had a coat for every goatly activity.

One for exploring, and one for climbing rocks. One for playing in the hay, and another for splashing in the rain.

Prospect even had a cape that made him feel like a SUPER goat. At night, he had a coat for dreaming.

Each time Prospect wore a new coat, his mom took a picture. The tiny goat pranced and posed. He was happy and warm and proud.

Soon, Prospect and his coats became famous. Everyone wanted to buy the little goat a coat. Packages came from all over the world!

With each passing day, Prospect got bigger, stronger, and more playful. His mom was so proud! She couldn't wait for Prospect to meet the other animals.

One sunny day, Prospect ventured outside.
First, he met a chicken. Then, he met the other goats.
They were so big. And their coats were so thick!
Prospect wondered how he would ever fit in.

Prospect decided he needed a special coat to impress the other goats. Would they like his blue jacket or his plaid cape?

But none of the coats fit Prospect. He had grown too much. The little goat was no longer little! Prospect sighed sadly and sprawled on a mountain of sweaters, jackets, and coats.

Prospect wanted to go outside and join the other goats, but he was nervous without his coat. Would they like him? Would they be nice?

Piney nudged Prospect toward the door. At first, the goat didn't move. But slowly, with another little nudge from Piney, Prospect put one hoof in front of the other.

Prospect was nervous as he approached the big goats. But as soon as the goats saw him, they gave a loud "meh" of approval. They loved his "new" coat.

Prospect's real coat had grown without him noticing. He was still a small goat, but now he stood tall and confident. Prospect realized he was wearing the most beautiful coat of all...his own!

The End

THE GOAT
WITH MANY COATS

The True Story

Hi, I'm Leanne Lauricella. People also call me "Goat Mama" because I rescue baby goats. I have a farm called *Goats of Anarchy* in New Jersey, where I care for more than 50 goats. Plus, we also take care of 2 lambs, 2 pigs, 6 dogs, chickens, a miniature horse, and a miniature donkey. We have a very full house!

Leanne

Meet Prospect. He was born just before Christmas, and he weighed only one pound. He was so tiny that it was hard for him to stay warm in the chilly weather.

So I did what any mom would do—I gave him a coat! Prospect loved his tiny coat. He loved it so much, in fact, that I started to dress him up in a different coat for every occasion.

He had a coat for rainy days, and one for sunny days too. One for windy days, another for snowy days, and one for especially cold days.

I took pictures of Prospect in his coats and posted them on Instagram. People loved it! Prospect started receiving coats from his fans all over the world.

Now Prospect had a coat for breakfast, a coat for lunch, a coat for bedtime, and a coat for nap time. He even had a coat for brushing his teeth!

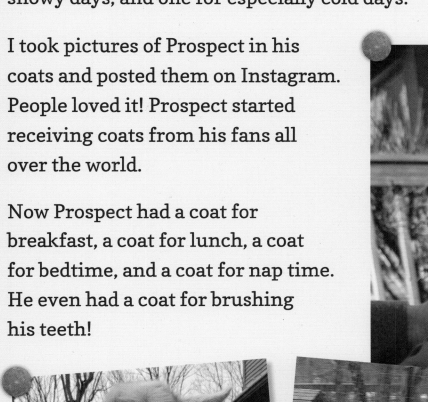

Prospect in his coats

Springtime came, and it was time for Prospect to meet the rest of the animals on the farm.

They all stared at him, wondering what he was wearing. None of the other animals wore coats!

But Prospect had a friend in Piney the pig. The two of them loved to spend time together, basking in the sun or snuggling up for a nap.

Prospect and Piney

As the weather grew warmer, and Prospect grew bigger, the tiny coats started to grow tighter. He still wanted to wear the coats he loved so much, but they just wouldn't fit him anymore!

Besides, as Prospect grew, he had the most beautiful coat of all—his own!

These days, Prospect has lots of friends on the farm to spend time with, including his best friend Piney. While he doesn't need to wear his coats anymore, he still puts one on every once in a while—just for fun!